CUTE KIDBITS

CUTE KIDBITS

Funny Conversations Kids Share With Their Pediatrician

JAY RABINOWITZ, M.D.

Parker Peds Publishing

Parker CO

ISBN: 9780692616055
ISBN: 0692616055

For all of the delightful children with whom I have had the opportunity to have conversations

Cute Kidbits

Kibitz—*Talking to someone in a friendly and informal way.*

   Kidbits—*Kids talking in friendly, informal, and often comical and embarrassing ways.*

   In the 1950s, during the Golden Age of television, a TV host named Art Linkletter had a show called "People are Funny". At one point during the show, he interviewed young children. He had a way of getting the kids to say some very humorous remarks. He coined the phrase "Kids say the darndest things".

   In the 1980's, and for the next 30 plus years, I've been "interviewing" children as a Pediatrician. They still say the darndest things, but the topics can be very interesting in a doctor's exam room. The dialogue can be amusing, often compelling or fascinating, entertaining, intriguing, certainly thought provoking, and often just plain amusing or charming. There can be excitement, or dread and fear. There can be good news (mainly), or bad (shots, mainly). Children may be well, but may be ill. But they all have something to say.

All of the quotes included in this book are verbatim--not changed in any way.

CONTENTS

1

WASTE MANAGEMENT

WHAT IS FUNNIER than toilet humor to kids? They have so many different names for what they excrete. When we ask them how those functions are performing, it always gets a laugh. And often an interesting comment. It is also not unusual to get an interesting response when we ask for a sample. Here are a few quotes that stand out. Try to hold it in!

Chapter 1
Waste Management

Doctor: "Do you use the potty?"

3 year old: "Yeah, but sometimes I use the hot tub."

When asked why he brought us out 2 cups of urine to be tested, a 12 year old responded, "I couldn't stop."

A 3 year old who had constipation remarked, "My butt's not working."

A 16 year old replied, while handing his urine sample cup to the nurse, "This Bud's for you."

When asked to give a urine sample, a 6 year old replied, "I took care of that at home, and I don't have anymore."

A 3 year old telling the doctor how he recently went on the potty for the first time: "I told dad to come over and see that big boy" (pointing to his BM).

When a 5 year old was asked to pee in the cup to obtain a sample, she replied, "Are you serious?!"

Doctor: "Have you experienced any positive effects after your tonsillectomy?"
15 year old: "Yeah, my poops are softer."

Doctor: "Are you ticklish."
4 year old: "I'm so ticklish that sometimes I pee."

2

Let's Embarrass Our Family

I REMEMBER THE time that my daughter, learning about the dangers of alcohol in 4th grade, informed her teacher that her dad was an alcoholic. This was because I had had a beer the night before while watching football with friends, and probably the only beer that I had all month. That set off a series of phone calls, and rather embarrassing since I was the local Pediatrician.

Kids will say what is on their minds, and parents have no clue as to what will come out of their mouths. It may not always be anywhere near accurate, but it gets attention. Nonetheless, it makes for some laughable moments.

Chapter 2
Let's Embarrass Our Family

When asked what polio drops tasted like, a 4 year old replied, "Like bourbon."

When a 4 year old was asked what he liked best to eat, he replied, "Peanut butter and jelly and sloppy nose."

A 5 year old proudly stated, "TV is my life--and candy too."

Doctor: "Do you wear your seatbelt in the car?"
9 year old: "Yes! All the time. My mom's driving scares me."

Doctor: "So you went to visit your gramma. What did she say?"
4 year old: "She said to come back later."

Doctor: "What do you like to eat?"
6 year old: "McDonald's, Wendy's, Burger King, KFC, and sometimes I eat junk food."

Doctor: "What are your jobs at home?"
6 year old: "Everything. I'm their slave."

A 3 year old who gets nebulizer treatments at home was asked by his grandma, "What do your parents do when you're sick?" The 3 year old replied, "They give me Budweiser treatments."

Nurse: "What did you get for Christmas?"
4 year old: "One bowling pin."

A 4 year old told us why his 7 year old sister was here, by saying, "She's sick with lettice-gitis."

As a 4 year old was crying loudly during the entire visit, her grandmother commented, "She sounds like an overpaid athlete."

Doctor: "What job do you do at home for mom or dad?"
8 year old: "I fix the TV when mom breaks it."

Doctor: "Do you help mom and dad with chores?"

5 year old: "Only mom. Dad lays around and eats chips."

5 year old: "We're going to watch a movie tonight."

Doctor: "What movie?"

5 year old: "Not sure yet. It's mom's turn to pick and she usually likes chicken flicks."

A 10 year old, after admittedly doing poorly in a race car video game while waiting in the exam room, said, "I guess you won't want me driving, huh, dad?"

5 year old, after getting 5 stitches in her knee: "My mom sews my clothes. Not this good though."

Doctor: "How is your family doing?"
5 year old: 'My mom has a baby in her tummy. She doesn't have a big tummy yet, but pretty soon it will be big like my dad's."

3

ALL EARS

NO MATTER HOW one tries, there is only one orifice in the body that we cannot see into--our ears. Maybe that is why they can be so mysterious to kids. What does it actually look like in there? How deep does the ear canal go? Does one have a lot of wax in there? Or animals? Or food? Of course, sometimes those ears will hurt, or ring, or just not seem right. Here are some kid's comments about those mystifying ears.

Chapter 3
All Ears

After having her ears cleaned, a 5 year old remarked, "Mommy, my ears are burping."

A 3 year old explained to the doctor, "My ears hurt; there's Teenage Ninja Mutant Turtles in there, and they're fighting."

When a 4 year old was asked why she was here, she replied, "I'm sick. My ears aren't working."

After the doctor playfully remarked to a 4 year old that he had potatoes growing in one ear and carrots in the other, the youngster snapped back, "And I've got broccoli in my nose."

A 3 year old who was having her temperature taken by the ear thermometer stated, "I think I hear my brains in there."

A 4 year old, when asked to describe how his ears felt, stated, "There is crunching in my ears--like bones."

A 4 year old who did not want to do his hearing test replied, "I can't do the hearing test because my ears are tired."

3 year old: "I have a horse in my ear."

Doctor: "How did it get there?"

3 year old: "It sneaked in and fell asleep."

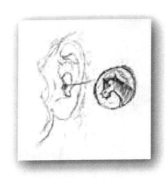

Doctor: "I understand that you have an earache."

3 year old: "No. But my ears hurt."

Nurse: "Do you have any booboos?"

5 year old: No, but I have fluff in my ears."

Said a 3 year old with an ear infection, "Someone shut my ear off last night and didn't turn it back on."

During a hearing test, a 5 year old was asked if she heard the high pitched beeps. She replied, "It sounds like 'low gas'." (Time to fill up the tank).

4

THOSE DARN 3 YEAR OLDS

AH, TO BE 3 again. Few worries, no deadlines, no homework. They can put sentences, paragraphs, and even stories together. Most speak rather clearly by then. They have enough language skills to be dangerous! And they are not afraid to speak their minds. They can be shy or outgoing, silly or serious, quiet or loud. They may have learned behaviors from siblings or preschool mates, or be completely innocent. They are almost always honest. And that is where some great quotes come from. They may not always speak in volumes, but these short responses should amuse you.

Chapter 4
Those Darn 3 Year Olds

Doctor: "Do you eat vegetables?"

3 year old: "Sure I do. My favorite one is macaroni."

Doctor: "How are you feeling?"

3 year old: "Old."

After a 3 year old fell off the exam table, he said, "That was awesome!"

Doctor: "I heard you had a birthday yesterday."

3 year old: "Yeah, but it's closed now."

Nurse: "You're a little hoarse."
3 year old: "No. I'm a little girl."

A 3 year old, who was having a wart treated, remarked, "I want you to kill the wart...but don't kill me."

Doctor: "Do you like to eat?"
3 year old: "Yes, I do. And I like to toot."

Doctor: "What are you looking forward to on your trip to California?"
3 year old: "Drinking out of juice boxes."

When a 3 year old's mom told him that if mommy was a girl then daddy was a boy, the 3 year old responded, "Daddy isn't a boy--he's a dude!"

A 3 year old stated, after handling the doctor's reflex hammer, "This is a hammer that does not ham."

Doctor: "What do you do with a spoon?"
3 year old: "Hang it on your nose."

A 3 year old, while throwing a tantrum, said, "We forgot to ask Santa what kind of cookies he likes."

Doctor: "I want you to give up your pacifier and also to begin to use the potty."
3 year old (with a shrug and turning his eyes up): "Whatever."

Nurse: "Let's have you stand on the scale."
3 year old: "I can't do that when I'm hungry."

Doctor, asking a 3 year old with a bean stuck up his nose: "So how did it get there?"
3 year old: "It must have jumped in."

5

SHOTS AND OTHER OUWIES!!

NOTHING STRIKES FEAR in a patient more than the word "shot". (And we are not just talking kids!). Although not everyone is afraid of them--some even ask to "bring it on"--each child wants to know if they are getting one (or more) that day. One can get knocked into the boards in hockey, tackled by a large hulk in football, fall off one's bike, or get slugged by a friend, but none of these events scare a person more than that 1 inch extremely thin needle. When the pressure is on, kids like to talk. Here is what they say.

Chapter 5
Shots and Other Ouwies!!

Doctor: "You'll be getting shots soon."

4 year old: "OK."

Doctor: "Do you know what that means?"

4 year old: "Yes, I'm getting ice cream."

After her five year old sibling just received her vaccine, a 3 year old cried vehemently, "I want one too."

While having his blood drawn, a 10 year old told this joke, "What is the name of Dracula's boat? The blood vessel."

A 3 year old, fascinated by a drop of blood on her finger after a finger prick, exclaimed, "It's doctor juice."

When asked by a nurse which arm she wanted her shot in, a 10 year old responded, "Either arm; just don't put it in the bone."

Mom, to a 4 year old who doesn't want his shots: "It will help you get bigger."
4 year old: "But I'll get big by eating my vegetables."

6 year old: "What are you wiping my arm with?"
Nurse: "It's just alcohol to clean it before your shot."
6 year old: "But alcohol is only for people over 21!"

Doctor: "There are no shots for you today."

3 year old: "Yeah!"

Doctor: "Do you know what shots are?"

3 year old: "No."

Dad: "Soon kids won't even cry after shots; they'll just text WAAAAAH."

5 year old: "It smells like shots in here."

Dad, after his 4 year old received 4 shots: "OK, time for you to go back to school. And me to go to the bar."

A 4 year old asked, "When you give me my shot, can you do it nicely?"

After a 4 year old received some shots, the nurse asked, "Would you like some water?"
The 4 year old replied, "No, because the water will come out the holes."

6

More From Those 3 Year Olds

THOSE 3 YEAR olds have so much to say that I needed to add another chapter. They seem so innocent and always speak what they believe to be the truth. They just do not always understand what they are saying, or at least adults do not grasp what they mean. But sometimes, actually, quite often, the results are hilarious.

Chapter 6
More From Those 3 Year Olds

While walking out the door after being examined, an ill 3 year old asked, "Am I better yet?"

During a 3 year old's developmental test, the doctor asked, "If an elephant is big, a mouse is…" The 3 year old replied, "Not big."

A 3 year old, as the doctor walks in the room, said, "Are you ready to operate?"

When asked what was wrong with her, a 3 year old replied, "I have a lot of garbage in my throat."

A 3 year old who was in the office for possible chicken-pox asked, "Do I have Kentucky Fried chickenpox?"

When a 3 year old was asked what he wanted to be when he grew up, he replied, "A pediatrician, so I can have toys."

After a mom told the doctor that a flu bug had been around the house, her 3 year old replied, "Yeah, and that bug is pinching my stomach."

When asked what her problem was, a 3 year old remarked, "I have a headache in my stomach."

A 3 year old said, "I hid your keys in a very special spot so you couldn't leave without me." Mom then asked, "Do you remember where you hid them?" "No", answered the girl.

A 3 year old told her mom, "I'm going to the pediachicken."

Replied a 3 year old when she asked why she was waking at night, "I hear my hair growing."

While the doctor was listening to a 3 year old's heart, the 3 year old asked, "Can you take it out for me?"
Doctor: "No."
3 year old: "It must be glued, right?"

A 3 year old diagnosed with strep replied, "I think cookies will help my throat."

7

LOGIC, ACCORDING TO A KID, PART 1

WHEN YOU ASK a kid a question, they almost always have a good answer. It all makes perfect sense to them. But it may cause the rest of us to think, "huh?" Kid's solutions are often very clever, thoughtful, or wise, but not always with the same logic as an adult. At any rate, it is often amusing and priceless, as you will see.

Chapter 7
Logic, According to a Kid, Part 1

After taking a whole handful of stickers, and being told by her mom that it was too many, a 2 year old replied, "No, mom, I have pockets."

Upon asking a 5 year old to define what a ceiling is, the reply was, "A place where balloons go."

As a 5 year old was asked to draw a picture of her father on a sheet of paper, she replied, while looking at her dad, "He's too big to fit on this paper."

When one of our staff asked a mother of three why only one of her children had red hair, her 6 year old replied, "He probably got it from our dog (a golden retriever)."

After being examined by the doctor, a 5 year old responded, "You haven't gotten me better yet."

When a 6 year old who was coughing was told by his mother to cover his mouth, he replied, "But I'll get germs on my hands."

When a 6 year old asked for her autograph, the nurse asked if she knew what an autograph was. The 6 year old replied, "It's your name, but a little sloppier."

A 4 year old, when asked by the doctor to touch the floor, in order to check his back, replied, "I am touching the floor--with my feet."

8 year old: "Why am I so tall?"
Doctor: "It's because of your genes."
8 year old: "No. I was tall before I got these pants."

When a 7 year old was told he had a virus, he replied: "I thought only computers get viruses."

Doctor: How do feel now that you are 4?"
4 year old: "Taller."

When a 9 year old was asked if he worried about anything, he replied, "Oh yeah! I worry a lot. That's why I have this wart. I'm a worry wart."

A 9 year old, when asked what she does for exercise, said, "I play piano. But that's just exercise for my fingers."

A 4 year old, after mom was told to put oil in his ears to loosen wax, remarked, "Are you going to put oil in my ears like daddy puts oil in his Jeep?"

A 4 year old, when told to take a baking soda sitz bath: "Am I going to turn into a cookie?"

8

LOGIC, PART 2

NOW THAT ALL made perfect sense--to them. Some may have made a joke of the question (showing a good sense of humor for their age), but most were honest replies. Here are some more logical explanations that you can ponder, or smile.

Chapter 8
Logic, Part 2

5 year old recently asked one of our staff: "How old are you?"

Staff: "60."

5 year old: "Did you start from 1?"

Doctor: "Why are you coughing?"
4 year old: "Because I talk too much."

Doctor: "What do you want to be when you grow up?"
11 year old: "I'd like to be an architect, but I'll probably be an orthodontist. You know, the big bucks."

Doctor: "What do you do if your clothes catch fire?"
6 year old: "Get some money and buy new ones."

Nurse: "Can you let your arm out so I can take your blood pressure?"
5 year old: "Sure. I worked out this morning."

When a 9 year old was asked what he was doing when he was having trouble breathing and shortness of breath, he replied, "I was writing really fast in school."

Doctor: "What do you want to be when you grow up?"
5 year old: "I'm going to be either a princess, or work at Home Depot."

Doctor: "So what happened to you today?"
6 year old: 'I fell off my scooter and hit my chin."
Doctor; "Did you have your helmet on?"
6 year old: 'Yes, but my mom didn't get me one with a chin strap."

Doctor: "Do you want a sticker?"
6 year old: "No, I don't like stickers, but I'll take money."

7 year old on why he doesn't want to use sunscreen: "I want to be a red neck."

Doctor: "What do you like best about preschool?"
4 year old: "Well, coloring makes me tired."
Doctor: 'Why does coloring make you so tired?"
4 year old: "Because I'm soooo good at it."

7 year old: "I wear knee pads, elbow pads, and a helmet when I ride my skateboard. Do you want to know why?"
Doctor: "Why is that?"
7 year old: "Because I'm not very good at riding my skateboard."

Mom: "What kind of food should he eat to help him get over this?"

Doctor: "No restrictions; he can just listen to his stomach and eat what sounds good."

5 year old: "You mean my stomach is going to talk to me?"

4 year old about his goals in life: "I'm trying to be sticky and stretch like Spiderman."

9

Just Too Cute

KIDS WILL SAY the cutest things. You may laugh, or maybe just say "ahhh". You may find some of these quotes charming and adorable. Some kids have already learned how to milk the system. But they are mostly honest. Just kids being kids.

Chapter 9
Just Too Cute

After the doctor told the parents of a 2 year old with sores on her mouth to use soothing ice cream, the 2 year old replied, pointing to the prescription pad, "Write that one down."

When a 4 year old who was playing with her toy phone was asked to come and get weighed, she replied into the phone, "Hold please."

When a 4 year old was being reminded not to talk to strangers, he remarked, "I never talk to strangers. (pause) Mom, what's a stranger?"

After a nurse explained to his parent which screening tests were to be done, a 6 year old asked, "What's a screaming test?"

When asked how he felt, a 5 year old replied, "I have a big virus."

When a 2 year old was asked if she was ready to see the doctor, she replied, "I'd rather go shopping."

Said a 2 year old with a diaper rash to the doctor, "I got a bad butt."

When a 12 year old girl, who was injured when running into a boy in gym class, was asked what the other kid looked like after the collision, she replied, "Well, he was sort of cute."

6 year old: "Vaseline is good for my lips, but not gasoline, right?"

Said a 6 year old, at his annual exam, to the doctor, "Quit the talking and let's get down to business."

A 2 year old walked on the scale and said, "Size me up."

A 2 year old remarked, "I think I have pink eye. Mom, where did my brown eyes go?"

4 year old: "Have you seen that movie Star Warts?"

Doctor: "Do you have a lot of friends at school?'
5 year old: 'Yes, and Justin is my boyfriend. I'm going to marry him."
Doctor: "Really?"
5 year old: 'Yes, but sometimes he acts like he's only a 2 year old."

Doctor: "What did you get for your birthday?"
2 year old: "Cake."

Doctor: "Have you gone anywhere this summer?"

4 year old: 'We went to the beach."

Doctor: 'Very nice. How was it?"

4 year old: "If the sand gets in your mouth, it's very crunchy."

At Thanksgiving, a nurse asked a 4 year old what part of the turkey he liked best. He answered, "The stomach (stuffing)."

Celebrating his birthday, a 5 year old proudly stated, "I've been fingers all my life, and now I'm a thumb."

10

SAY AGAIN?

DID HE (SHE) just say that? Was I hearing that correctly? When kids remark on topics, their answers may be concise and confident. But they may not always make sense to someone else immediately. Read some of these over again if you need to. If you can stop laughing.

Chapter 10
Say Again?

As her infant brother was being weighed, a 5 year old asked, "Can I get weighed to see how old I am."

After discussing water safety, a 5 year old replied, "Now that I know how to swim, I don't drown anymore."

After reminding mom that her 6 year old was allergic to sulfa, he replied, "Mom. You mean I can't sit on the sofa anymore?"

While the doctor was moving his stethoscope around while listening to a 5 year old's heart, the 5 year old remarked, "Can't find it, huh doc!"

An 8 year old stated, "I'm growing bigger, but my bike is growing smaller."

When a 5 year old was being weighed on the scale she asked, "Have I gotten to the fat section yet?"

A 4 year old described a stuffy nose by saying, "I'm having a heart attack in my nose."

When asked why she was at our office, a 6 year old replied, "I was playing and a rock fell in my nose."

After our nurse said to a 5 year old girl who had just coughed, "Oh, you're a little hoarse," the youngster replied, "No, I'm a little girl."

A 2 year old stated, "Mommy, I can hear my nose talking."

When a 4 year old was asked what was bothering her, she pointed to her swollen neck glands and replied, "These balls in my throat."

Doctor: "You're sick and need some medicine."
4 year old: "Well I'm sick of medicine."

A 5 year old was asked if he felt well for his check up that day, and he replied, "I think there is something wrong with my teeth--I can't eat meatloaf."

Doctor: "If you have a bad dream, try not to go into your parent's room."
6 year old: "OK. I'll just call you."

Doctor: " You must be Kyle."
Kyle: "Yeah. And this is my mom, but my dad calls her Marilyn."

When asked if he had any hobbies, a 5 year old replied, "I collect money."

Doctor: "How old are you?'
Patient: "5 years old."
Provider: "And how long have you had the cough?"
Patient: "20 years."

Doctor: "Do you speak English?"
5 year old: "No. Spanish." "Can I have 2 stickers?" (In perfect English)

11

TEENAGERS

TEENS--SOMETIMES THEY act like adults, and sometimes they act like kids. Their remarks are like that too. It is not just little ones who give the best lines. Teens can be funny too. Or wise guys just looking for a laugh. Either way, believe what you want, these teens really said these.

Chapter 11
Teenagers

Doctor to a 15 year old who failed his vision test: "Can you even see the blackboard?"

15 year old: "I can see the blackboard. I just can't see the letters."

Doctor: " Do you see a dentist regularly?"
14 year old: "Yes. My father."

Nurse: "Did you take any medicines in the past 24 hours?"

15 year old: "Yes. That cough-cold, horrible tasting, totally disgusting, ineffective, that didn't help at all medicine."

Teen: "What's up doc?"

Doctor: "You must be a Bugs Bunny fan."

Teen: "Who?"

Teenager, remarking on the Colorado weather: "Why is it so bipolar here?"

Doctor: "How much sleep do you get every night?"

16 year old: "Usually 15 or 16 hours."

Doctor: "Wow. What do you do the rest of the day?"

16 year old: "Since I don't go to sleep until 3 am, I'm really only awake in the evening."

When the doctor asked a teenager how school was going, he replied, "It's ok, except the classes get in the way."

Mom, to her teenage son who was ill and had to stay home, "This is your punishment--you have to watch daytime television."

Nurse: "Do you have any medication allergies?"
13 year old: "Yeah, anything injected with a needle."

Doctor: "What do you do for exercise?"
15 year old: "I'm a competitive video gamer."
Doctor: "How about anything that gets your heart beating faster and gets you tired?"
15 year old: "Tired? You try gaming for 8 hours straight."

Doctor: "How are things going at school?'
Mom: "He has a good relationship with his teacher."
13 year old: "It's not like I'm dating her."

12

COMPLIMENTS

SOMETIMES KIDS WILL say things that are just too nice to pass up. They may not be funny, but they are sincere. They say it from their hearts. There is no hidden agenda here. Just sweet talking. Sometimes they compliment others, and sometimes they just like to compliment themselves. Here are a few compliments.

Chapter 12
Compliments

A 3 year old remarked, "Doctor, I think I sure love you."

A 2 and ½ year old proudly exclaimed to the entire office, "I'm potty trained now."

One child's answer to the question, "How old are you?" was "Two and precious."

After her appointment, a 3 year old said to the doctor, "Thanks for joining us."

Doctor (extending hand): "It's nice to meet you."
3 year old: "Yeah, I already have friends."

As the doctor was leaving the room, a 4 year old said, "It was a pleasure having a well visit with you today."

13

SIBLING RIVALRY

SIBLINGS OFTEN COME along for the ride when one has to go to the doctor. Of course, they are often looking for an opportunity to stick it to each other. They love to comment or critique, especially when they are not the one being the patient that day. But they can be very funny too. Here are some examples of that.

Chapter 13
Sibling Rivalry

When a 4 year old was asked if she was going to watch the nurse give her younger sibling a shot, she exclaimed, "I want to give the shot!"

Responding to an 11 year old's complaints of sore throat, cough, and congestion, the doctor asked, "So it sounds like the cough is bothering you the most?" Interjected his 8 year old sister, "No, I bother him the most."

A 6 year old boy describing his younger sister: "She's OK on the surface, but she can get on your nerves if you live with her."

When the doctor asked a 7 year old with a cold if he blew his nose, his 10 year old brother answered, "No, but he picks it."

Younger brother to older sister: "You can't have shingles--they go on the roof of the house."

Doctor: "Do you fight with your brother?"
6 year old: "Yes, but I'm trying to quit."

After an 8 year old identical twin was examined, she remarked, "You don't need to examine my sister; she looks just like me."

2 year old: "I have a rash."

Doctor: "Do you think your brother has it too?"

2 year old: "No, it's a girl rash."

When the doctor questioned a 1 year old, "Are you ill?", her 3 year old sister promptly replied, "She's not ill; she's Kristen."

A 3 year old who was in with her sibling, but wanted to be examined too stated, "I'm so glad I'm sick."

14

Got To Love Throat Cultures

WE HAVE SHOWN how kids hate shots. But throat cultures rate right up there in the "yukky" category. It is one thing getting gagged; it is another when you are getting gagged with a sore throat. Of course, kids have lots to say about these. They also have numerous ways to describe the feeling in their throats. Here are a few comments of what they have to say.

Chapter 14
Got To Love Throat Cultures

A 6 year old getting a throat culture asked, "Are you going to terrorize my throat?"

After sticking the tail of a toy dinosaur down the throat of another, a 4 year old commented, "Look, he's getting a throat culture."

Just before a throat culture was to be performed, a 2 year old stated, "Thank you, but I'm not sick today."

A 3 year old who was about to have a throat culture asked, "Are they going to swallow my throat?"

A 4 year old remarked, "My throat's not sore. I don't want the stick (tongue depressor), I just want the paper (the prescription)."

After receiving a throat culture, a 4 year old said to his mom, who was helping to hold him down: "You're fired."

A 6 year old, about to get a throat culture, asked, "Do you have to use the stick--my breath's not red."

A 3 year old with a sore throat remarked, "I have rocks in my throat."

3 year old with a sore throat: "I have a throat in my mouth."

4 year old with a sore throat: "My teeth are biting my throat."

Doctor: "The strep test was negative."

6 year old: "So I went through that (the throat culture) for nothing?"

15

AGAIN, SAY AGAIN?

YOU HAVE HAD a few chapters to digest what the kids said in chapter 10. Sometimes you have to read the quote over again, as you think, "huh?" Here are some more "clearer than mud" quotes.

Chapter 15
Again, Say Again?

Doctor: "What is your favorite food?"

5 year old: "Chocolate."

Doctor: "What food group is that in?"

5 year old: "Candy."

Doctor: "Do you want to take medicine for your allergies?"

12 year old: "No. I'll just keep breathing out of my mouth."

Doctor: "My, it looks like you've grown a foot since I've seen you."
5 year old (looking down at her feet): "No, I still only have 2."

Nurse: "What is your favorite food?"
5 year old: "Fish."
Nurse: "What kind of fish?"
5 year old: "Fish that swim in the water."

Doctor: "What is your job to help mommy and daddy?"
4 year old: "Staying out of the way."

Doctor: "What sports do you do?"
6 year old: "Wii sports."

Nurse, asking parent about safety, "Do you have ATV's?"

5 year old interrupts: "No, but we have direct TV."

Nurse: "Did you go on any trips this summer?"

5 year old: "I tripped on the sidewalk."

Doctor: 'So what are you going to do now?" (after the exam)

8 year old: "I'm going to party like a rock star."

Doctor: "Do you have any pets?"

4 year old; "We had 2 dogs, but one died."

Doctor; "Oh, I'm sorry."

4 year old: "Well we didn't kill it!"

7 year old: "Can I listen to my heart too?"

Nurse: "Sure. Here's my stethoscope."

7 year old: "Ahhh man. Is it going to smell like a doctor?"

Doctor: "What did you eat for lunch today?"

4 year old: "Graham crappers."

After a mom said to our nurse that she wasn't sure how sick her daughter was, and that the visit may be fruitless, the 7 year old remarked, "I'm not fruitless. I eat pears every day for lunch."

Doctor: "I'm going to prescribe you a cough syrup."

7 year old: "Can I use it on pancakes?"

16

I've Got To Get Undressed?!

YOU KNOW KIDS will comment on this topic. After all, they are told never to get undressed for anyone, except parents. Or maybe doctors too. But some areas need exposure to be examined accurately, and that means clothes off.

Chapter 16
I've Got To Get Undressed?!

A 12 year old, when putting on her pink exam gown, stated, "I look like a Pepto Bismol."

Doctor: I'm going to examine you now. Take off your clothes."

5 year old: "Lock the doors!"

Doctor: "Why don't you take off your shirt so I can do your check up?"

5 year old (looking over to his mom): "Mom, why don't you take off your shirt too!"

Doctor: "Take off your shirt so I can listen to your chest."

6 year old: "Is this for real?"

Doctor: "Take off your clothes to be examined."

4 year old: "You want to see me naked, huh?"

A 12 year old, while wearing a gown for her exam, stated, "I feel like a napkin."

Doctor, after the exam: "The nurse will be back in shortly."

5 year old: 'Does that mean I have to get naked again?"

17

A FINAL QUOTE

EVERY PEDIATRICIAN PROBABLY has that one absolutely funny story that beats all of the rest. I do too. When I tell it, others say they haven't laughed that loud in ages. The story is absolutely true, and innocent, but salty.

Let me set it up. I was seeing a 5 year old girl for her annual physical. Her mother and 3 year old brother accompanied her that day. I had known the family for some time. Mom was very prim and proper; that day she was wearing a long white dress. The 5 year old was very sweet and behaved. But the 3 year old was another story. Let us say, a bit on the active side. We were in an exam room with windows looking out onto a busy four lane road.

As I was talking with mom and the 5 year old, 3 year old brother was all over the place, interrupting frequently. I thought I would distract him by asking him to look out the window and tell me if he sees any trucks.

Little did I know, though, that he had a speech impediment--"tr" came out as "f".

Almost immediately, he blurted out "_uck". "There goes another _uck." Wouldn't you know it--it was like a caravan of trucks passing by the window at that time. "_uck, another _uck, a big _uck". And so on.

Mom was getting very embarrassed by this time. I was going to just make a cute comment, but knew how conservative and reserved she was. I just chose to try to finish as quickly as I could, and pretend I was not hearing him.

But then a dump truck drove by, and the 3 year old yelled loudly and excitingly, "Look, a dum _uck!"

ACKNOWLEDGMENTS

I HAVE HAD the privilege to meet thousands of wonderful patients and their families during my many years in practice. I thank them for their trust, but also their fabulous quotes.

I have also had the honor of working with countless magnificent staff, including many who helped collect these quotes.

I particularly wish to thank Rich Hayes, a physician assistant associate, and photographer, who took the brilliant pictures included in the book.   Also, thanks to his daughter, Lexi, for her fun sketches sprinkled throughout the book.

Thank you to my friend Debra Fine, author of <u>The Fine Art of Small Talk</u> series, for guiding me on how to get a book published.

Finally, thanks to all of my friends and family, who encouraged me over the years to put these precious quotes in a book so that others can share the joy.

Made in the USA
Charleston, SC
05 November 2016